Children's
FIRST
Book of

HUMAN BODY

Children's

FIRST

Book of

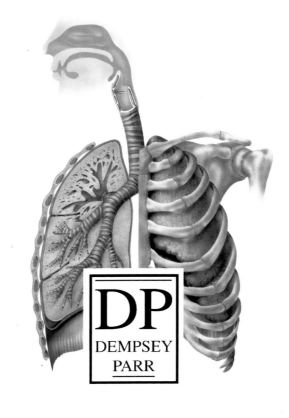

DP
DEMPSEY
PARR

Author and Editor
Neil Morris

Projects created by
Ting Morris

Art Direction
Full Steam Ahead Ltd

Designer
Branka Surla

Project Management
Rosie Alexander

Artwork commissioned by
Branka Surla

Picture Research
Rosie Alexander, Kate Miles, Elaine Willis, Yannick Yago

Editorial Assistant
Lynne French

Additional editorial help from
Suzanne Airey, Hilary Bird, Jenny Sharman

Editorial Director
Jim Miles

The publishers would like to thank the following people for their help:
Jenni Cozens, Pat Crisp, Ian Paulyn, Matthew Tew

This edition published by Dempsey Parr, 1999
Dempsey Parr is an imprint of Parragon

Parragon

Queen Street House

4 Queen Street

Bath BA1 1HE, UK

Copyright © Parragon 1998

Produced by Miles Kelly Publishing Ltd
Bardfield Centre, Great Bardfield, Essex CM7 4SL

ISBN 1 84084 471 X

Printed in Spain

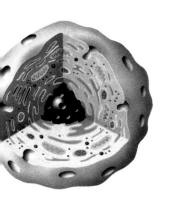

Contents

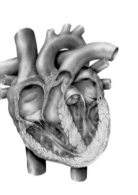

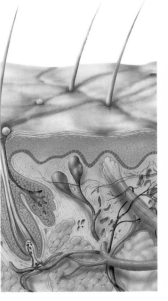

How to use this book

In this book, every page is filled with information on the sort of topics that you will enjoy reading about.

Information is given in photographs and illustrations, as well as in words. All the pictures are explained by captions, to tell you what you are looking at and to give even more detailed facts.

A New Words box appears on every double-page spread. This list explains some difficult words and technical terms.

Project boxes describe craft activities related to the topic. These are things to make or simple experiments to do. The photograph helps to show you what to do, and is there to inspire you to have a go! But remember, some of the activities can be quite messy, so put old newspaper down first. Always use round-ended scissors, and ask an adult for help if you are unsure of something or need sharp tools or materials.

Illustrations are clear and simple, and sometimes they are cut away so that you can see inside things.

Caption triangles point to the right picture. Other captions starting with a symbol give extra pieces of information that you will find interesting.

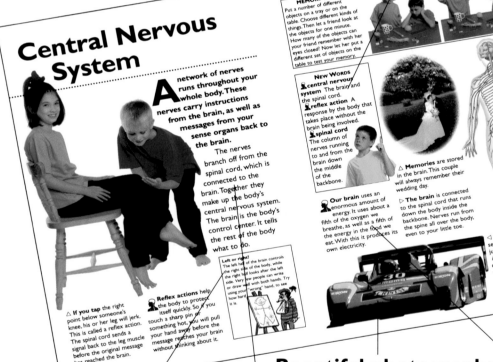

The cartoons throughout the book are not always meant to be taken too seriously! They are supposed to be fun, but the text that goes with them gives real information.

Beautiful photographs have been specially chosen to bring each subject to life. The caption triangle points to the right photograph.

The main text on each double-page spread gives a short introduction to that particular topic. Every time you turn the page, you will find a new topic.

Human Body

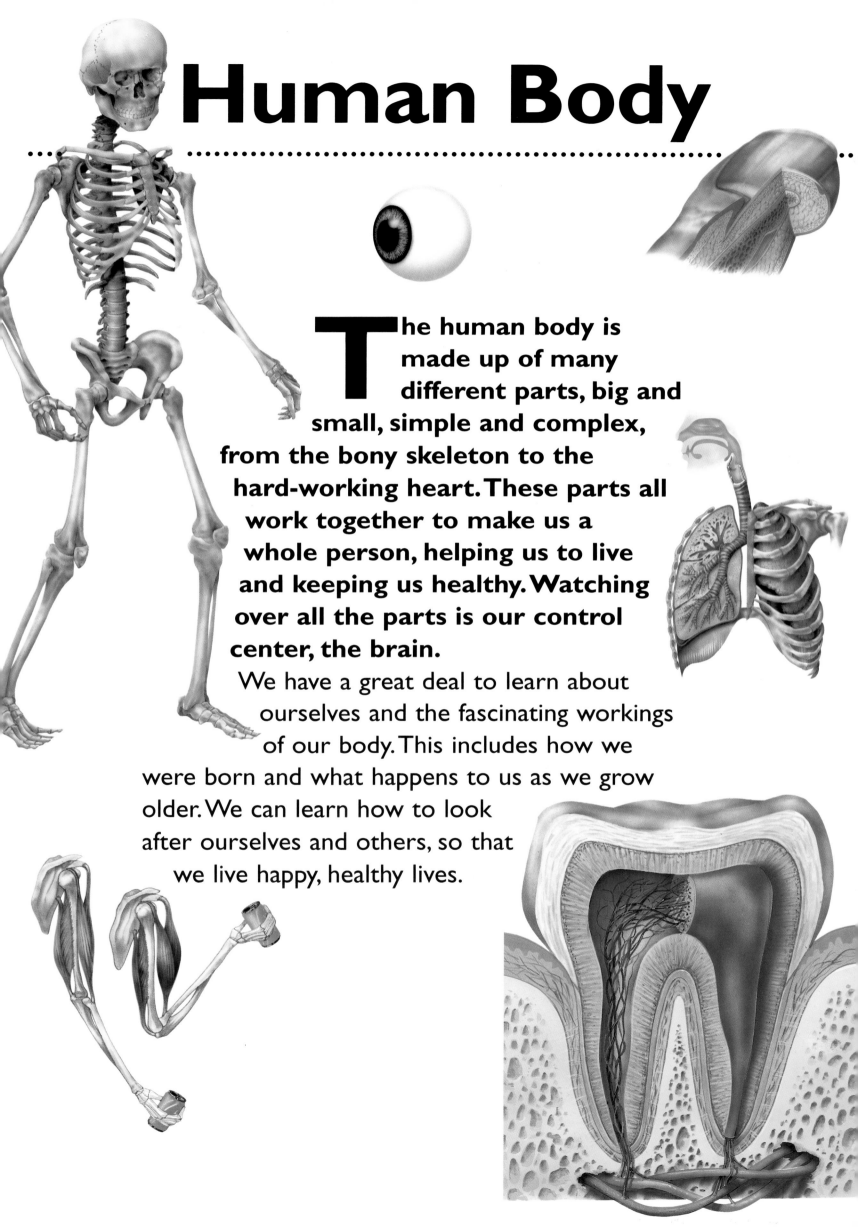

The human body is made up of many different parts, big and small, simple and complex, from the bony skeleton to the hard-working heart. These parts all work together to make us a whole person, helping us to live and keeping us healthy. Watching over all the parts is our control center, the brain.

We have a great deal to learn about ourselves and the fascinating workings of our body. This includes how we were born and what happens to us as we grow older. We can learn how to look after ourselves and others, so that we live happy, healthy lives.

Parts of the Body

head

hand

neck

arm

torso

Men and women, boys and girls are all human beings. Our bodies are all similar, though no two people look exactly the same.

The human body is made up of many parts, each having its own special job to do. These different parts are all controlled by the brain, which also enables us to think and move. Our senses of sight, hearing, touch, taste, and smell help us in our daily lives. Our bodies need energy to make it work, which we get from our food.

Two thirds of your body's weight is made up of water. It also contains carbon, calcium, and iron.

◁ **The largest part** of the body is called the torso, or trunk. The four limbs are joined to the torso. The hands at the ends of our arms help us touch and hold things. Our feet help us stand upright and walk. The head is on top of the neck, which can bend and twist. The brain is inside the head.

leg

foot

NEW WORDS

brain The control center of the body, which also lets us think.

limb An arm or a leg.

nucleus The central part of a cell.

tissue Groups of similar cells that are joined together to form parts of the body.

torso The trunk of the human body, from below the neck to the top of the legs.

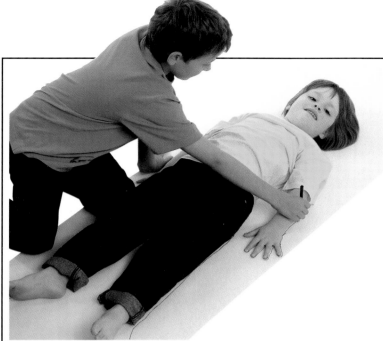

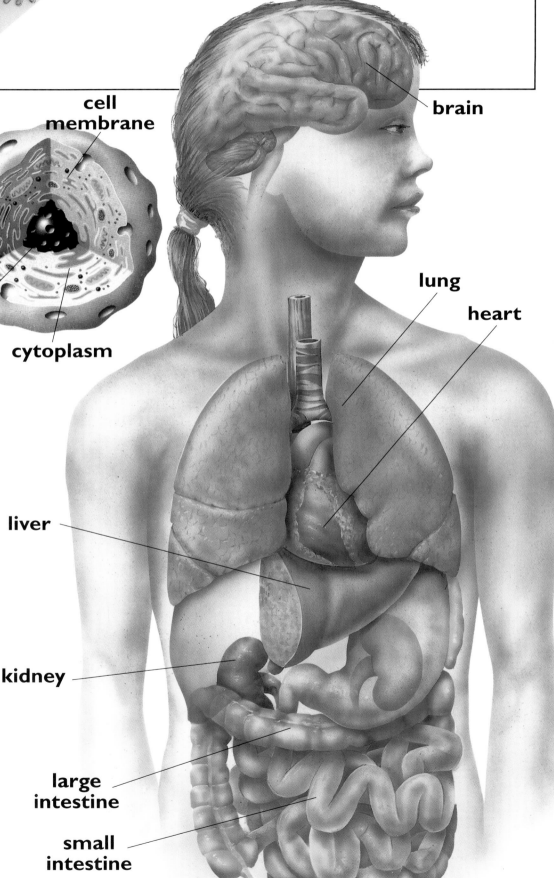

brain

lung

heart

cell membrane

nucleus

cytoplasm

liver

kidney

large intestine

small intestine

▷ **All parts of the body** are made up of tiny living units called cells. Every body contains billions of cells, so small that they can only be seen through a microscope. Most cells have three main parts. In the middle is a nucleus, the control center that helps make new cells. This is surrounded by a soft fluid called cytoplasm. The outer surface of the cell is called its membrane.

We all begin life as one single cell. This divides into two, these cells also divide, and so on. Similar types of cells join together to make tissue.

▷ **We have many large organs** inside our bodies. These are parts that do special jobs for the rest of the body. Organs work together to make up different body systems.

Skeleton

The skeleton is our framework of bones. Our bones provide a firm surface for muscles to attach to, helping us to move.

The skeleton also protects our body's organs. The skull protects the brain. Our heart and lungs are protected by the rib cage. The body's bones vary in shape and size. The places where they meet are called joints, which is where muscles move bones.

skull

humerus

rib

vertebra

ulna

pelvis

radius

spongy bone — marrow — compact bone

periosteum

◁ **At the center** of bones is soft marrow. This is inside the toughest part, called compact bone, which is lined with spongy bone. A bone's outer layer is called the periosteum.

femur

▷ **33 vertebrae** make up our spine, or backbone. At the bottom is the pelvis. A woman's pelvis is wider than a man's, to make room for a baby. The lower parts of our arms and legs have two bones. The femur, or thigh bone, is the largest bone in the body.

tibia

fibula

10

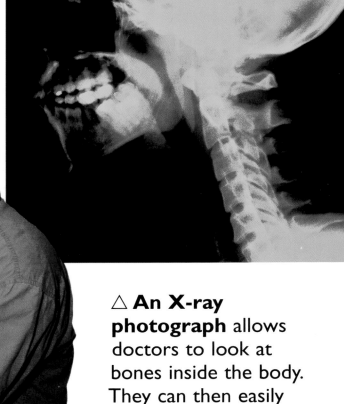

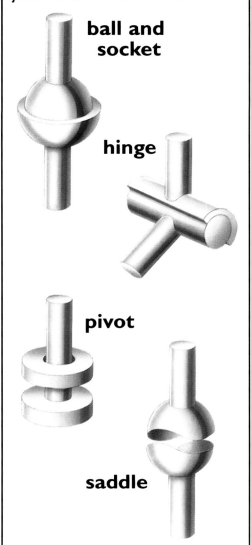

MOVING JOINTS

Joints let us move in different ways. The hip and shoulder are ball-and-socket joints. The knee and elbow are hinge joints. There is a pivot joint at the top of the spine, a saddle joint at the thumb's base.

ball and socket

hinge

pivot

saddle

An adult has about 206 bones. Babies are born with as many as 270 small, soft bones. As a child grows, some of the bones join together.

You may be up to half an inch shorter in the evening than early in the morning. The weight of your upper body squashes your spine slightly as you stand and walk during the day.

▽ **For broken bones** to heal properly, they have to be placed next to each other and kept still. That is why a doctor puts a broken arm or leg in a plaster cast. New bone tissue grows to join the broken bone ends together again.

△ **Insects,** such as this beetle, have their skeleton on the outside of their body. It acts like a shell, covering and protecting the soft parts underneath. It also protects the insect from its enemies.

△ **An X-ray photograph** allows doctors to look at bones inside the body. They can then easily see if a bone has been broken or damaged.

11

Muscles

All our movements, from running and jumping, to blinking and smiling, are made by our muscles. The muscles do this by becoming shorter and pulling the bones to which they are attached.

The human body has about 620 muscles that it uses for movement. In addition there are many more that work automatically. These include the muscles that make the heart beat, the chest muscles that help us breathe, and the stomach muscles that help us digest food.

chest muscles

bicep

abdominal muscles

sartorius

▷ **The body** is moved by several layers of muscles. There are large muscles near the surface under the skin, and others lie beneath them. Three layers of criss-crossing abdominal muscles connect the rib cage to the pelvis. The body's largest muscle is in the buttock.

▽ **More than 30 small muscles** run from the skull to the skin. These allow us to make facial expressions, which we use to show our feelings.

happy

shocked

sad

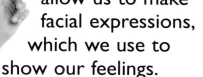

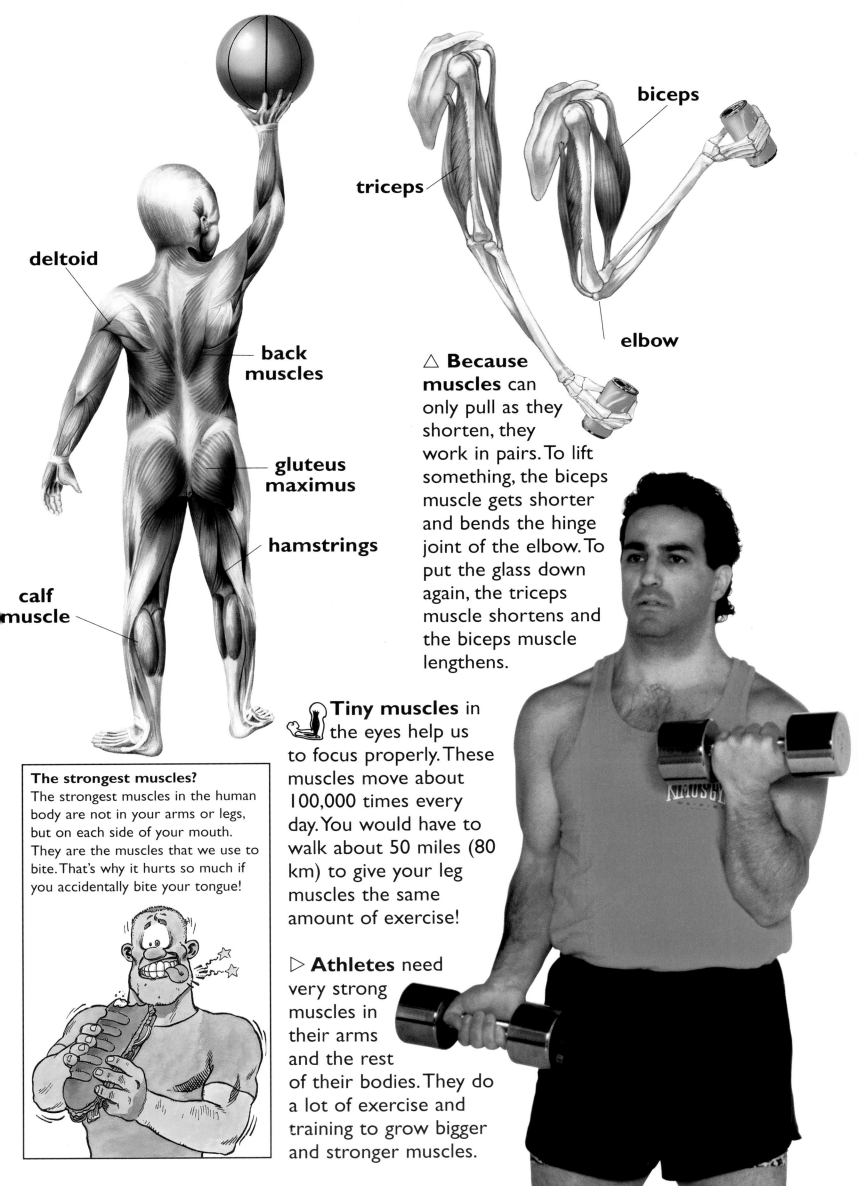

deltoid

back muscles

gluteus maximus

hamstrings

calf muscle

triceps

biceps

elbow

△ **Because muscles** can only pull as they shorten, they work in pairs. To lift something, the biceps muscle gets shorter and bends the hinge joint of the elbow. To put the glass down again, the triceps muscle shortens and the biceps muscle lengthens.

Tiny muscles in the eyes help us to focus properly. These muscles move about 100,000 times every day. You would have to walk about 50 miles (80 km) to give your leg muscles the same amount of exercise!

▷ **Athletes** need very strong muscles in their arms and the rest of their bodies. They do a lot of exercise and training to grow bigger and stronger muscles.

The strongest muscles?
The strongest muscles in the human body are not in your arms or legs, but on each side of your mouth. They are the muscles that we use to bite. That's why it hurts so much if you accidentally bite your tongue!

The Heart and Blood Circulation

heart

artery

vein

The heart is a powerful muscle that pumps blood all around the body. The blood carries oxygen from the air we breathe and goodness from the food we eat.

The heart is pear-shaped and is about as big as your clenched fist. It lies in your chest, behind your ribs and just to the left of the bottom of your breastbone. If you put your hand on your chest near your heart, you can feel it beating. A child's heart rate is about 100 beats a minute. When you are running or if you are very active, your heart beats faster and your body's cells then need more oxygen and food.

Hold one hand up and the other down for one minute.

△ **Blood** travels away from the heart in blood vessels called arteries. It travels back to the heart in veins. In the illustration, arteries are red and veins blue.

▷ **Your heart** has to work harder to pump blood upward, because then it is working against gravity. If you hold one hand up for a minute, you'll see that it has less blood in it afterward than the other hand.

14

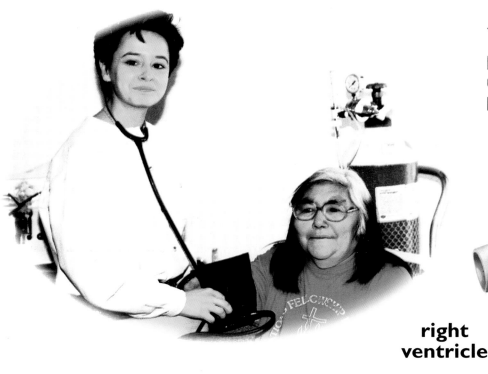

▽ **The right side** of the heart pumps blood to the lungs to pick up oxygen. The left side pumps the blood around the body.

aorta

right ventricle

left ventricle

△ **A doctor** can use a special instrument to measure blood pressure. The instrument squeezes, but it isn't painful. Having high blood pressure can put an extra strain on a person's heart. because it has to work harder.

An adult body contains about 10 pints (5l) of blood. So every day an adult's heart pumps over 14,000 pints (7,000l) of blood around the body.

LISTEN TO THE BEAT

You can make your own stethoscope, so that you can easily listen to your own or a friend's heartbeat. Simply cut the top end off two plastic bottles. Then push the ends of some plastic tubing into these two cups. Put one cup over a friend's heart and the other cup over your ear.

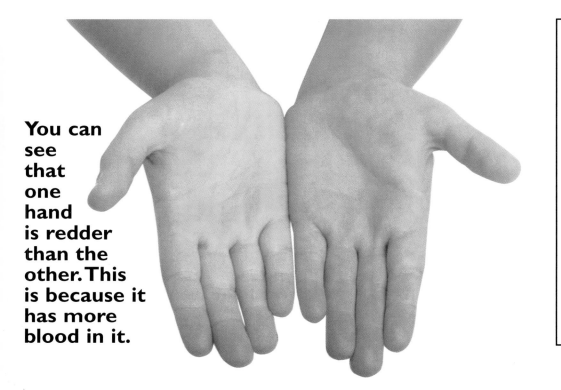

You can see that one hand is redder than the other. This is because it has more blood in it.

NEW WORDS

artery One of the tubes that carries blood away from the heart to all parts of the body.

stethoscope A doctor's instrument used for listening to sounds in a person's body.

vein One of the tubes that carries blood to the heart.

◁ **Runners** need to get a lot of oxygen to their muscles very quickly. To achieve this, they breathe hard and their hearts beat quicker. That's why you sometimes feel out of breath when you've been running.

An adult's lungs contain around 300 billion tiny blood vessels, called capillaries. If laid end to end, they would stretch over 1,200 miles (2,000 km).

asthma An illness that makes breathing very difficult.
capillary A very small blood vessel.
diaphragm A dome of muscle that separates the chest from the abdomen.
windpipe The tube through which air passes from the throat to the lungs.

We can't breathe underwater, so divers carry oxygen tanks on their backs. On the surface, they use snorkels. There is no air in space, so astronauts also carry backpacks of oxygen.

△ **This photo** of part of a lung was taken under a microscope, which magnifies it many times. The network of small passages inside the lung make it look and act rather like a sponge.

▷ **As you breathe in,** your rib cage expands and a large dome of muscle, called the diaphragm, flattens. When you breathe out, the diaphragm rises.

BREATH TEST
Fill a large plastic bottle and half-fill a large bowl with water. Cover the bottletop with your finger and turn it upside down in the bowl. You will find that the water will stay in the bottle. Take a plastic tube and carefully put one end of it into the neck of the bottle, under the water. Now everything is ready for the breath test. Blow hard into the free end of the tube. How much water can your breath push out of the bottle?

Breathing

Every time we breathe, we take in air containing a gas called oxygen. We need oxygen all the time to make our bodies work.

The air we breathe in passes into the two lungs, which are well protected inside the rib cage. The lungs take oxygen from the air and pass it into our bloodstream. Our blood takes oxygen all around the body.

When we breathe out, the lungs get rid of used air. Adults breathe about 18 times a minute, which is more than 25,000 times a day. Children usually breathe even faster.

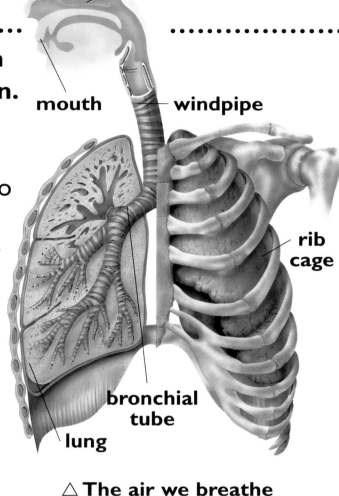

nasal cavity

mouth   windpipe

rib cage

bronchial tube

lung

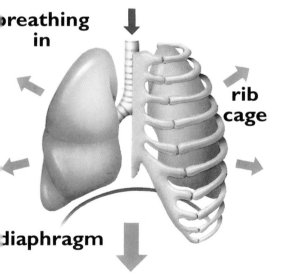

breathing in

rib cage

diaphragm

▽ **People who suffer from asthma,** or other breathing difficulties, often use an inhaler to help them breathe. The inhaler puffs a drug down into the windpipe. This makes the air passages wider and they can breathe more easily.

△ **The air we breathe** in through the nose and mouth goes down the windpipe. This branches into two bronchial tubes, one for each lung. Inside the lungs, the tubes divide and get smaller. Oxygen passes from the tiniest tubes to blood vessels and finally into the blood-stream.

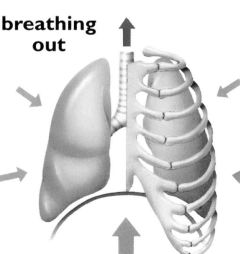

breathing out

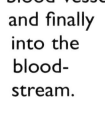

Making Sounds

We make sounds when we talk. We can whisper very quietly. We can laugh, scream, and sing. All the sounds that come out of our mouths are made in the throat.

Sounds are made by things vibrating, and your voice comes from vibrating vocal cords. These cords are soft flaps in the larynx, or voice box. They lie across the windpipe, behind the Adam's apple at the front of your throat.

To make loud sounds, we breathe hard over the vocal cords. If you put your hand on your throat and shout, you can feel the vocal cords vibrating.

WHISTLING
When people whistle, they force air through a narrow opening at great speed. The air is squeezed so that it vibrates and makes a high-pitched sound—a whistle.

◁ **We use our lips** and tongue to change sounds from our vocal cords and form words. There are a thousand different languages in tropical Africa alone. This Masai man speaks one of them.

▽ **Our vocal cords** move to make different sounds. Tiny muscles pull the cords together. When the cords are completely open, air moves freely past them and no sound is made.

closed

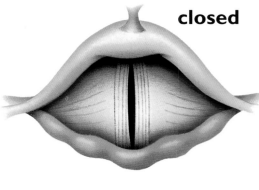

open

NEW WORDS

Adam's apple The lump at the front of the neck.

airway Air passage between the nose and the lungs.

larynx The voice box, containing the vocal cords.

vocal cords Flaps in the throat that can vibrate and then make sounds.

When we cough, we release air at a speed approaching 60 mph (100 kph), trying to remove something that is irritating our airways.

The vocal cords are specially designed to work and make sounds when air passes over them from below. But you can make them work when breathing in too. Try saying "hello" as you breathe in. It's like talking backward!

Do you snore?
You'll have to ask someone else for the answer to this question, unless you've ever woken yourself up by snoring very loudly. The noise is actually made by the soft part of the roof of the mouth vibrating. This can sometimes happen with such force that the loudest snores can make as much noise as a loud saw or even a pneumatic drill!

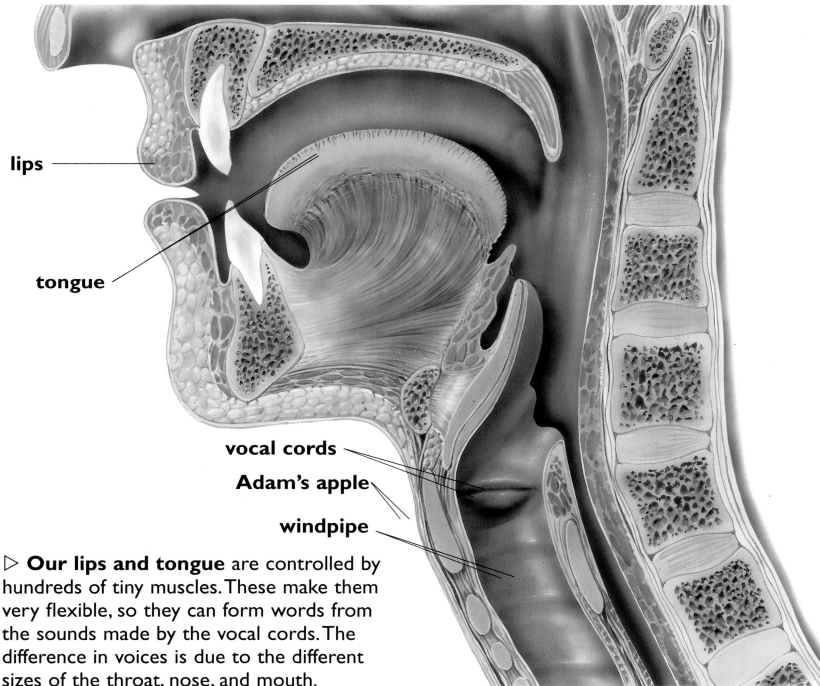

lips

tongue

vocal cords

Adam's apple

windpipe

▷ **Our lips and tongue** are controlled by hundreds of tiny muscles. These make them very flexible, so they can form words from the sounds made by the vocal cords. The difference in voices is due to the different sizes of the throat, nose, and mouth.

Central Nervous System

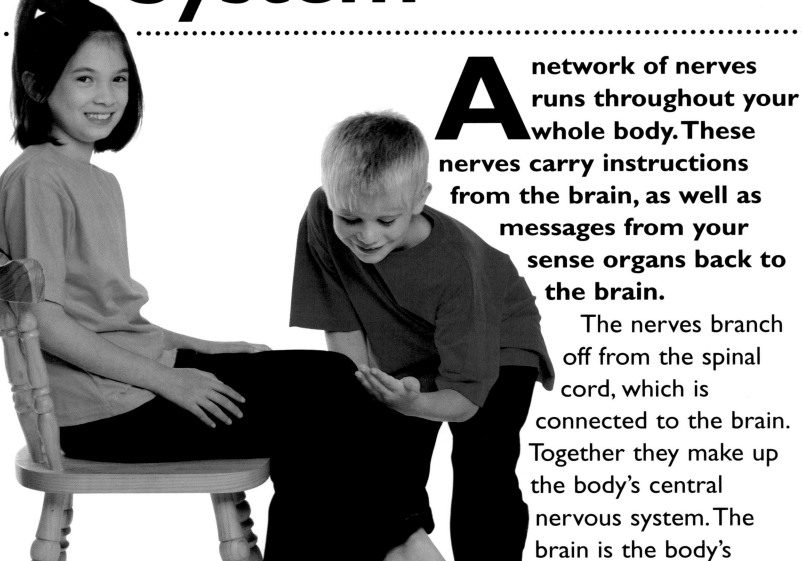

A network of nerves runs throughout your whole body. These nerves carry instructions from the brain, as well as messages from your sense organs back to the brain.

The nerves branch off from the spinal cord, which is connected to the brain. Together they make up the body's central nervous system. The brain is the body's control center. It tells the rest of the body what to do.

△ **If you tap** the right point below someone's knee, his or her leg will jerk. This is called a reflex action. The spinal cord sends a signal back to the leg muscle before the original message has reached the brain.

Reflex actions help the body to protect itself quickly. So if you touch a sharp pin or something hot, you will pull your hand away before the message reaches your brain without thinking about it.

Left or right?
The left half of the brain controls the right side of the body, while the right half looks after the left side. Very few people can write or draw well with both hands. Try using your "wrong" hand, to see how hard it is.

NEW WORDS

central nervous system The brain and the spinal cord.

reflex action A response by the body that takes place without the brain being involved.

spinal cord The column of nerves running to and from the brain down the middle of the backbone.

△ **Memories** are stored in the brain. This couple will always remember their wedding day.

Our brain uses an enormous amount of energy. It uses about a fifth of the oxygen we breathe, as well as a fifth of the energy in the food we eat. With this it produces its own electricity.

▷ **The brain** is connected to the spinal cord that runs down the body inside the backbone. Nerves run from the spine all over the body, even to your little toe.

◁ **Our brain** helps us to see and hear, as well as to judge speed and distance. A racing driver needs to combine all of these abilities very quickly. His brain sends messages to his hands and feet to steer and control the car.

Sleep

Sleeping takes up a lot of our time. Some people need more sleep than others, but most people spend about a third of their lives asleep.

We grow when we are asleep, so babies need at least 18 hours of sleep every day. Most children sleep for about 12 hours each night, and as we grow less, we sleep less. Most adults sleep for between six and nine hours a night. Many old people need very little sleep.

Sleep gives the body time to rest. Our muscles have very little work to do when we are asleep, and so the parts of the brain that control movements can rest too. Our reflexes are still at work, however, so we might brush away a fly in our sleep without even realizing.

We often sleep a lot more than usual when we are ill. We do this to give our body plenty of time to rest and mend itself. When we are well again, we long to get up!

We breathe more slowly when we are asleep, and our heart beats more slowly too. This means that all the different parts of our body are getting lots of rest.

△ **You may think** that you lie perfectly still at night, but you don't. People change their position many times during sleep. This is more restful for the body. If you stayed in one place all the time, your body would ache in the morning.

What is sleepwalking?
Some people sleepwalk: they get up and walk around while they are asleep. They don't know they are doing it, and they usually don't remember anything about it when they wake up the next morning.

NEW WORDS
infectious Quickly spreading to others.
nightmare A frightening dream.
sleepwalk To get out of bed and walk around while you are still asleep.

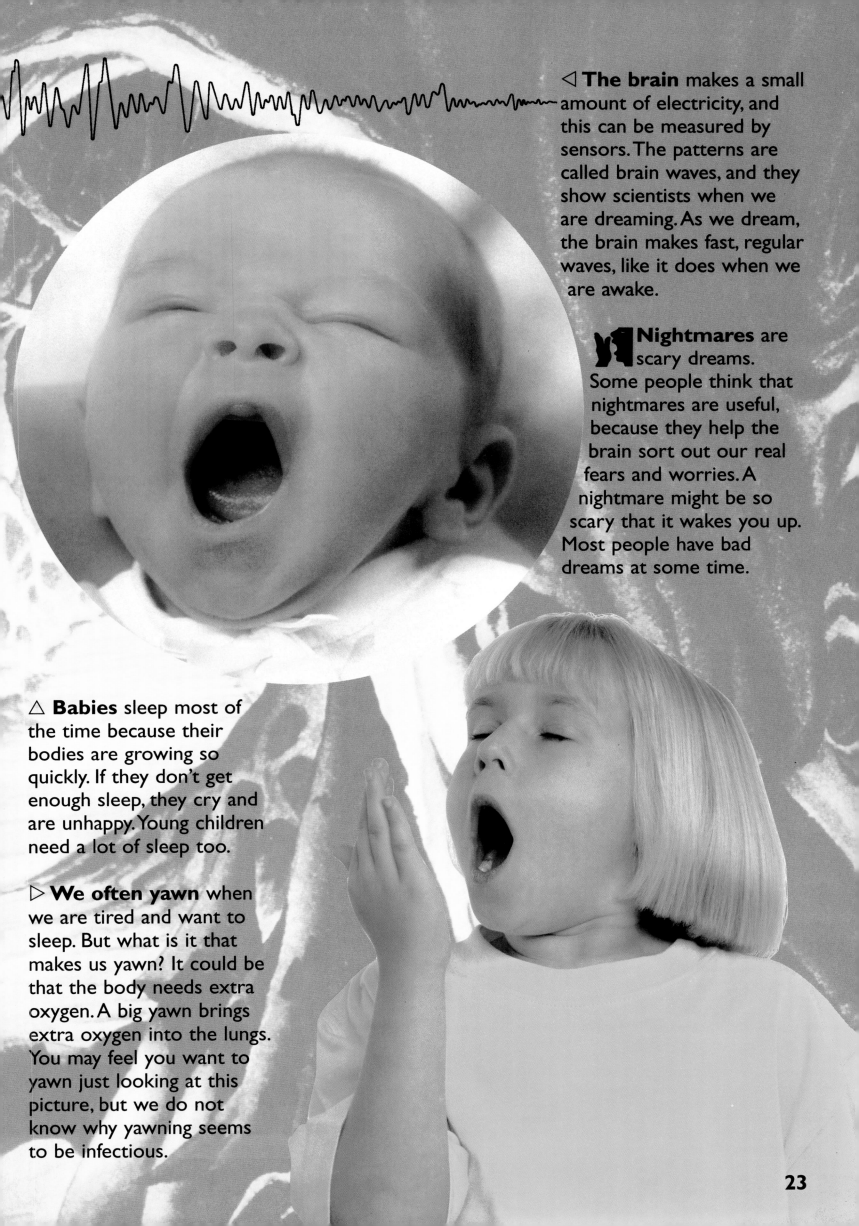

◁ **The brain** makes a small amount of electricity, and this can be measured by sensors. The patterns are called brain waves, and they show scientists when we are dreaming. As we dream, the brain makes fast, regular waves, like it does when we are awake.

Nightmares are scary dreams. Some people think that nightmares are useful, because they help the brain sort out our real fears and worries. A nightmare might be so scary that it wakes you up. Most people have bad dreams at some time.

△ **Babies** sleep most of the time because their bodies are growing so quickly. If they don't get enough sleep, they cry and are unhappy. Young children need a lot of sleep too.

▷ **We often yawn** when we are tired and want to sleep. But what is it that makes us yawn? It could be that the body needs extra oxygen. A big yawn brings extra oxygen into the lungs. You may feel you want to yawn just looking at this picture, but we do not know why yawning seems to be infectious.

23

straight hair

wavy hair

curly hair

△ **Hairs** grow from follicles, in the dermis. Different-shaped follicles make people's hair straight, wavy, or curly.

No two fingerprints are the same. Every person in the world has their own special pattern. That's why fingerprints can be used to identify people.

◁ **People sweat** when they are hot, so athletes sweat more on a very hot day. Sweat takes heat from the body and helps cool you down as it dries on your skin.

COMPARE PRINTS

It's best to wear some old clothes and put down lots of newspaper for this activity. It can be a bit messy! Use a roller or a brush to cover your fingers or your whole hand in paint. Then press down firmly on a sheet of paper. This will leave fingerprints and perhaps a whole hand print. When you have finished, compare your prints with a friend's. Are the prints the same? You could try looking at them through a magnifying glass—you'll really see the difference.

The Skin, Hair, and Nails

nail

half-moon

cuticle

fat

bone

skin

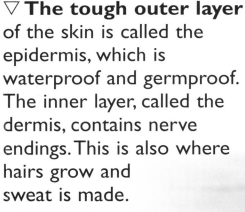

Skin protects the body and controls its temperature. It keeps out dirt, water, and germs, shields us from the Sun's burning rays, and stops the body drying out.

△ **Nails** are made of a tough substance called keratin. New nail grows from the base, under the skin. The pale half-moon is nail that has just grown.

Our skin is full of nerve endings, so it can send messages to the brain about things such as heat, cold, and pain. The skin produces nails to protect the tips of fingers and toes. It also makes hairs for extra warmth and protection.

▽ **The tough outer layer** of the skin is called the epidermis, which is waterproof and germproof. The inner layer, called the dermis, contains nerve endings. This is also where hairs grow and sweat is made.

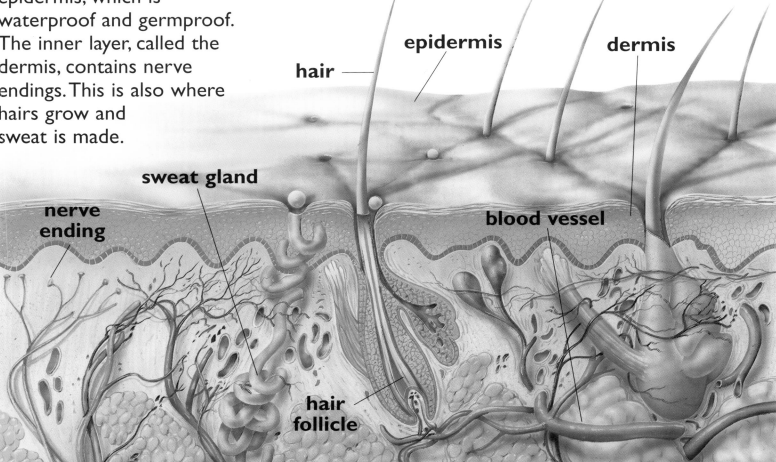

hair

epidermis

dermis

sweat gland

nerve ending

blood vessel

hair follicle

Teeth

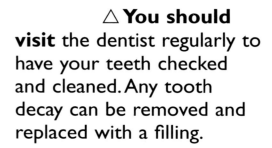

Our teeth are there to break food down into small pieces, ready for swallowing. The teeth have three different shapes, designed to do different jobs.

The incisors at the front are for biting into food and cutting it up. The pointed canines tear tough food. And the big molars at the back grind and mash it.

Children lose their first set of teeth, known as baby, or milk teeth, which start to fall out when we are five or six. A set of new, bigger teeth grows in their place.

▽ **The outside of the tooth** is a hard layer of enamel. The center of the tooth, with blood vessels and nerves, is surrounded by a substance known as dentine.

△ **You should visit** the dentist regularly to have your teeth checked and cleaned. Any tooth decay can be removed and replaced with a filling.

If sugar and bacteria are left on the teeth for long, they can produce acid. This breaks down enamel and causes tooth decay. Regular brushing removes the sugar and bacteria.

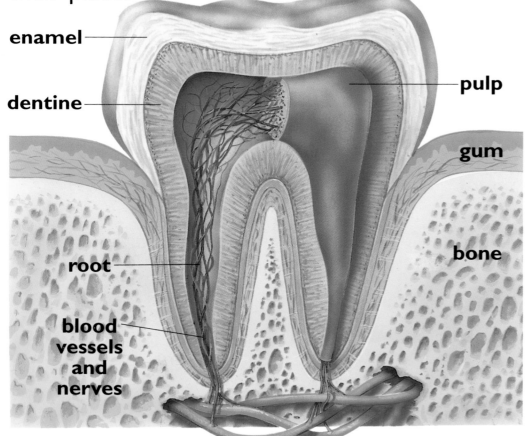

enamel

dentine

pulp

gum

root

bone

blood vessels and nerves

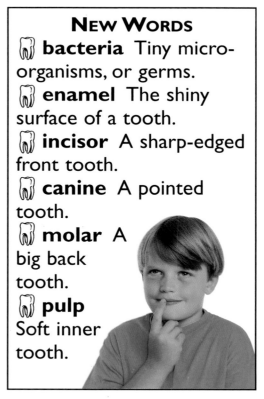

NEW WORDS
bacteria Tiny micro-organisms, or germs.
enamel The shiny surface of a tooth.
incisor A sharp-edged front tooth.
canine A pointed tooth.
molar A big back tooth.
pulp Soft inner tooth.

CHECKING YOUR TEETH

Plaque is a filmy deposit on the surface of teeth that causes decay. You can check how much plaque there is on your teeth by chewing a disclosing tablet (from a drugstore), made of vegetable dye. Plaque shows up as a deep pink color. Brushing your teeth well and regularly will mean less plaque and so less tooth decay.

When old people lose their teeth, they sometimes replace them with false teeth.

▽ **When you are small,** you have 20 baby teeth, shown in the inner circle. These are replaced by 32 permanent teeth, including four back wisdom teeth.

It has been known for people to grow a third set of teeth, but this is very rare indeed.

▽ **It is important** to look after your teeth well when you are a child, so that they will be healthy and strong when you are older. Some children and young adults wear braces for some time. This helps to make crooked teeth straight. Your dentist will tell you if this is a good idea.

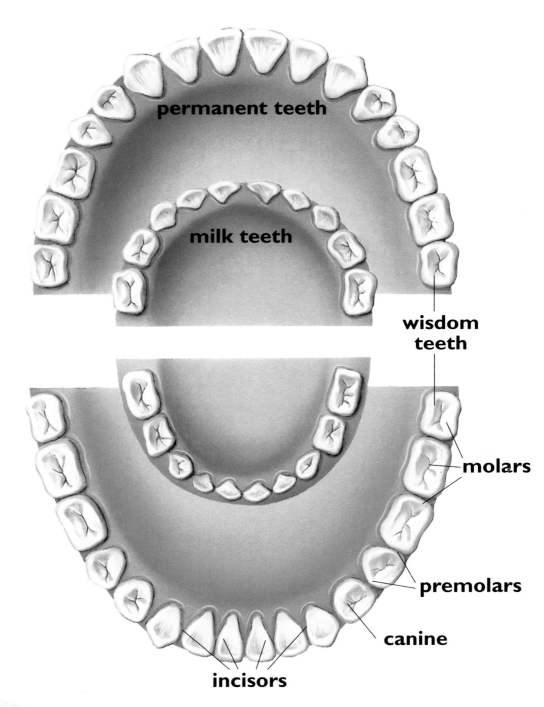

permanent teeth

milk teeth

wisdom teeth

molars

premolars

canine

incisors

△ **The four wisdom teeth** come through last, after the age of about 17. Some people never have wisdom teeth.

Our back teeth grind up our food, which mixes with saliva and goes soft and mushy. This makes it much easier to swallow and digest.

Digestion

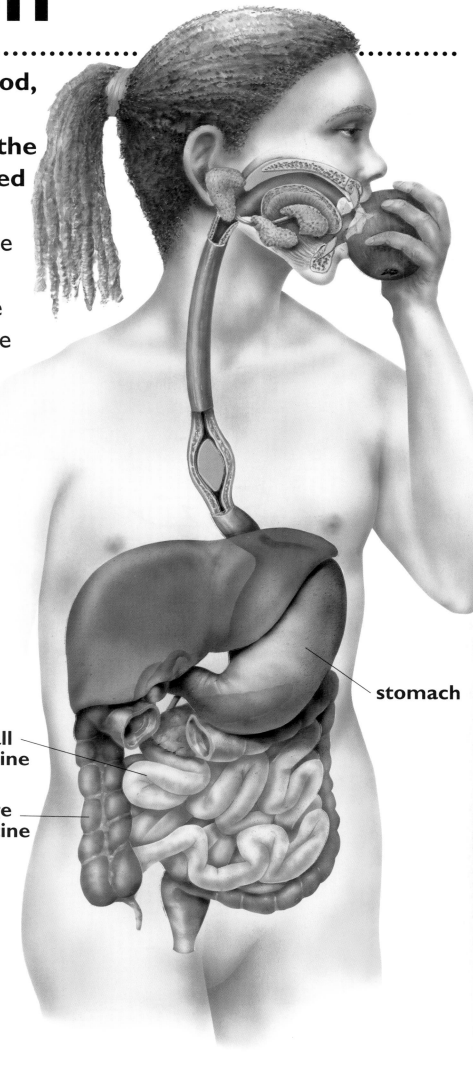

After we swallow food, it travels down a muscular tube to the stomach. There it is mashed into a souplike mixture.

The mixture passes into the small intestine, where tiny particles of food pass into the bloodstream. What's left of the food passes into the large intestine, and then waste products leave the body.

▷ **Digestion** takes up to 18 hours, from biting the apple to tiny particles of it passing into the bloodstream. Food stays in the stomach for three hours.

stomach

small intestine

large intestine

NEW WORDS

digestion The process of breaking food down and passing it into the bloodstream.

large intestine The wide tube where water is removed from the waste products of food.

small intestine The tube where food passes to the bloodstream.

villi Bumps in the small intestine.

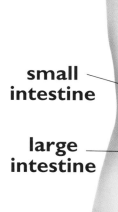

28

▷ **When we play,** we use up a great deal of energy. We need to eat and digest food to provide our body with that energy.

▽ **In the large intestine,** water is taken out of the parts of food that our body cannot use. The water becomes urine and the rest is solid waste. These pass out of the body when we go to the toilet.

△ **Inside the small intestine** are fingerlike bumps, called villi. These contain blood vessels that take the useful substances from food into our bloodstream. Blood, pumped by the heart, takes the energy from food to all parts of the body.

The small intestine is made up of over 16 feet (5 m) of coiled-up tube. It is longer than the large intestine, but the large intestine is much wider.

Food and Drink

We need energy to live, and we get that energy from what we eat and drink. Our bodies need important substances, called nutrients, that we get from food. They help us grow and repair damaged cells, as well as providing energy.

Different foods are useful to us in different ways. It is important that we don't miss out on any of the essential nutrients. To have a balanced diet, we must eat foods from various groups—carbohydrates, proteins, fats, and fiber, also vitamins and minerals.

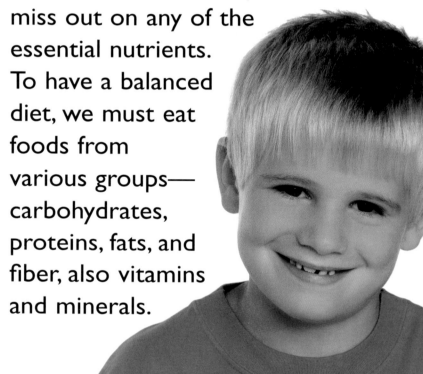

△ **Cereals and vegetables** are good to eat because they contain a lot of fiber. This is very useful because it helps other foods pass more easily through the digestive system.

The body needs small amounts of minerals, such as calcium and sodium. Calcium is needed for healthy bones and teeth. Milk contains calcium, as well as water, fat, protein, and vitamins.

◁ **Oranges** and other fruit contain a lot of Vitamin C, which keeps us healthy and helps us recover from illness. The body needs many other vitamins too.

▽ **Fats** such as cheese, butter, and milk are full of energy, as well as important vitamins. Fats can be stored by the body to use later, but it is not good to eat too many fatty foods.

△ **Beans and meat** contain lots of proteins, which help us stay strong. They are also used to make body cells, so they help us grow and stay healthy.

▽ **Carbohydrates,** such as bread and pasta, give us a lot of the energy that we need for our daily lives. We can make use of this type of energy very quickly.

Why do we need water?
The body uses water in many ways. Water helps to make up our blood. It keeps us cool by making sweat. It carries wastes from the body in urine. We get water from other drinks too, as well as from many different kinds of food.

HOME-MADE GRANOLA
Put 2 cups oats, 3/4 cups raisins, and 1/2 cup chopped nuts, along with some sunflower seeds, in a mixing bowl. Mix all the ingredients together. Then put your granola in a screw-top jar. Label the jar, adding the date. You can eat your granola with milk, yogurt, or fresh fruit juice, and have a healthy breakfast.

Smell and Taste

Smell and taste are important senses. Our sense of smell is much stronger than our sense of taste. When we taste food, we rely on its smell and texture to give us information about it as well.

We use our noses for smelling things. Tiny scent particles go into the nose with the air. The nose then sends messages through a nerve to the brain, which recognizes the smell.

The tongue also sends nerve signals to the brain about tastes. When we eat something, the tongue and the nose combine to let the brain know all about that particular food.

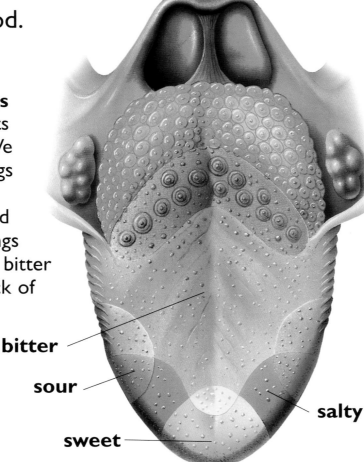

▷ **We taste different things** on different parts of the tongue. We taste sweet things at the tip, salty things just behind the tip, sour things at the sides, and bitter things at the back of the tongue.

bitter

sour

sweet

salty

△ **Flowers** give off a pleasant scent, to attract insects. A skunk can make a very nasty smell when it wants to scare off enemies.

When you have a cold and your nose is plugged, you can't smell much and you can't taste your food properly either.

Why do we sneeze?
We sneeze to help clear our noses of unwanted particles, such as dust. When we sneeze, the explosive rush of air from the lungs can reach a speed of 100 mph (160 kph)—as fast as a sports car!

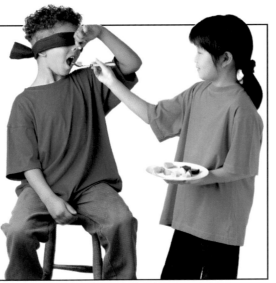

Most people can identify about 3,000 different smells.

▽ **This photo** of taste buds was taken through a microscope. Our tongue has about 10,000 taste buds, which pick up the four basic tastes and pass the information on.

NEW WORDS

mucus A moist, sticky substance in the nose.

olfactory nerve A nerve that runs from the nose to the brain, taking messages about smells.

particle A very very small piece of something.

taste bud A sense organ on the tongue that helps us taste things.

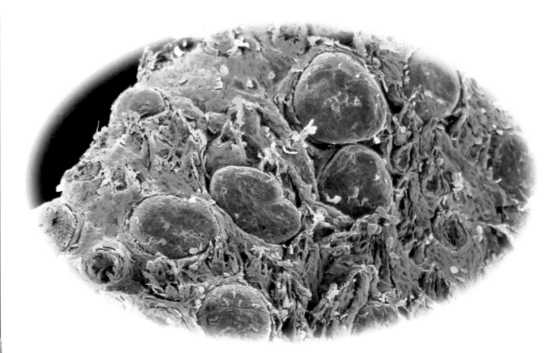

Babies have taste buds all over the inside of their mouths. They are also very sensitive to smells. As we grow older, our sense of smell gets weaker.

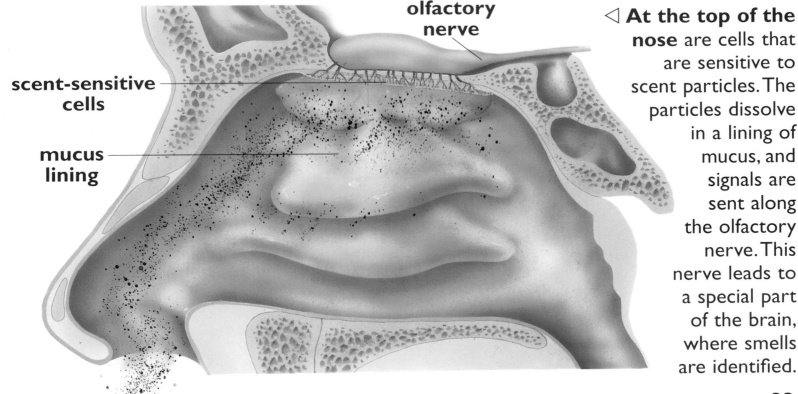

olfactory nerve

scent-sensitive cells

mucus lining

◁ **At the top of the nose** are cells that are sensitive to scent particles. The particles dissolve in a lining of mucus, and signals are sent along the olfactory nerve. This nerve leads to a special part of the brain, where smells are identified.

33

Hearing

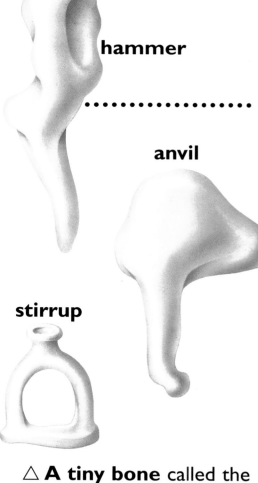

hammer

anvil

stirrup

When we look at someone's ears, we see only a part of them. This part, called the outer ear, is shaped to collect sounds as they travel through the air.

All sounds are made by things vibrating. Sound waves make the eardrums and other parts vibrate. Information on vibrations is then sent to the brain, which lets us hear the sounds.

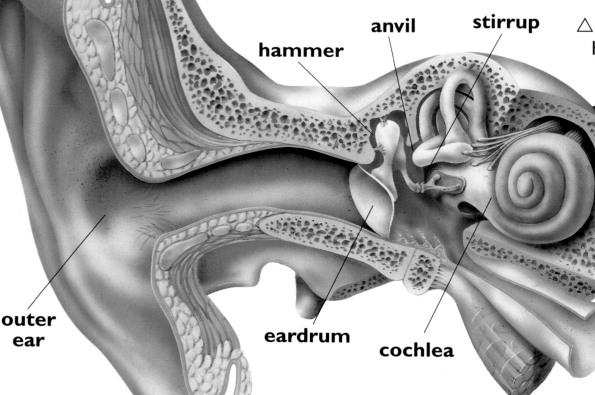

hammer

anvil

stirrup

outer ear

eardrum

cochlea

△ **A tiny bone** called the hammer is connected to the eardrum. The eardrum vibrates the hammer. The hammer then moves the anvil, which in turn moves the stirrup bone. Finally, the stirrup vibrates the cochlea.

△ **Sounds** pass into the ear and make the eardrum vibrate, which in turn vibrates tiny bones. The bones shake a spiral tube shaped like a snail shell, called the cochlea. Inside the cochlea is a fluid, which moves tiny hairs that send signals to the brain. Then we hear the sounds.

EARDRUM DRUM

To make a pretend eardrum, cut a large piece from a plastic bag. Stretch it over the top of a big can and hold it in place with a rubber band. Sprinkle some sugar onto the plastic. Then hold a metal tray near to it and hit the tray with a wooden spoon. The grains of sugar will jump about as your drum vibrates with the sound.

▽ **An old-fashioned ear trumpet** worked by acting as a bigger outer ear and making sounds louder. Modern hearing aids have tiny microphones and speakers.

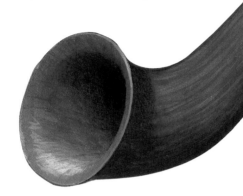

NEW WORDS

auditory nerve A nerve that carries messages from the ears to the brain.

cochlea A spiral tube in the inner ear, where vibrations are changed into nerve signals.

eardrum A fine sheet of skin inside the ear, which vibrates as sound waves hit it.

Have you ever felt your ears pop in a plane or an elevator? This sometimes happens when air pressure outside changes and is equalized in the middle ear.

▽ **Sounds travel well** through liquids, so it is easy to hear when you are underwater. Whales and other sea creatures make sounds to communicate with each other.

△ **Three canals** next to the cochlea, in the inner ear, help us keep our balance. They let the brain know what movements the body is making. Ballet dancers need excellent balance.

Seeing

We use our eyes to see. Rays of light come into each eye through an opening called the pupil, which is in the middle.

A lens inside each eye then bends the light very precisely, so that it travels to an area at the back of the eye called the retina.

The light rays make an image on the retina, but the image is upside down. Nerves send information on the image to the brain, which lets us see it the right way up.

▽ **Our eyes** are about the size of table-tennis balls, but we only see a small part at the front when we look in the mirror. The pupil is surrounded by a colored iris, which has a clear protective shield in front of it, called the cornea.

cornea

lens

pupil

iris

△ **Most people see** things in color, but some are color blind. This is a test card for color blindness. Can you see the shape inside the circle?

▷ **The color** of our eyes is really just the color of the iris. We inherit this color from our parents, and the most common color is brown. If one parent has blue eyes and the other brown, their child will usually have brown eyes.

▷ **Many people** wear glasses or contact lenses to help them see better. These change the direction of light before it enters the eyes, so that it focuses better on the retina.

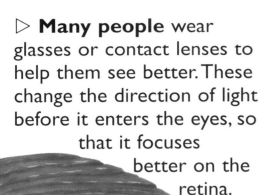

Why do we blink?
Our eyes make tears all the time. Tears are useful because they keep the cornea at the front of the eye damp. When we blink, it spreads the tears across the eyes. This keeps the eyes clean and stops them from drying out.

optic nerve

retina

day

night

NEW WORDS

cornea The clear protective layer that covers the pupil.

iris The colored part of the eye surrounding the pupil.

pupil The opening at the front of the eye that lets in light.

retina The layer at the back of the eye that is sensitive to light.

△ **When it is sunny or a bright day,** our eyes do not need to let in much light, and our pupils are small. But when there is less light, like at nighttime, the pupils have to open more and they get bigger. Small muscles change the size of the iris around the pupil.

About one in every 12 men find it very difficult to tell the difference between some colors, especially red and green. Very few women are color blind.

You blink about 15 times each minute, without thinking about it. The brain controls many actions such as this automatically.

37

▷ **Blind people** can read and write using a system called Braille. The letters of the Braille alphabet are a system of raised dots, which can be felt and understood through the fingertips.

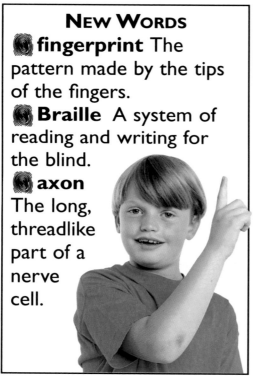 **The Braille alphabet** was invented by a Frenchman named Louis Braille (1809-1852). He went blind at the age of three, and later became an organ player and a professor.

▷ **Every person's fingertips** have a different skin pattern, called a fingerprint. These are the main fingerprint patterns.

arch   **loop**   **whorl**

NEW WORDS

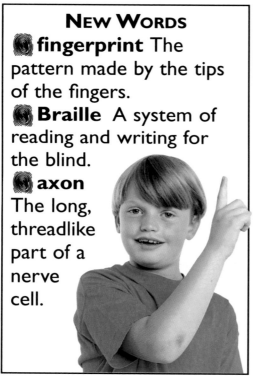 **fingerprint** The pattern made by the tips of the fingers.

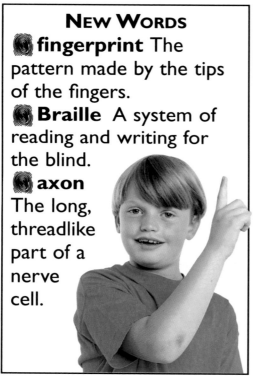 **Braille** A system of reading and writing for the blind.

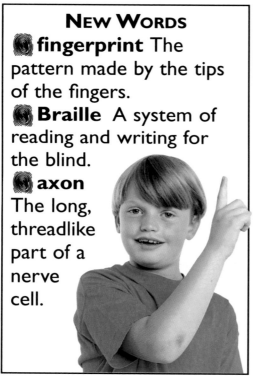 **axon** The long, threadlike part of a nerve cell.

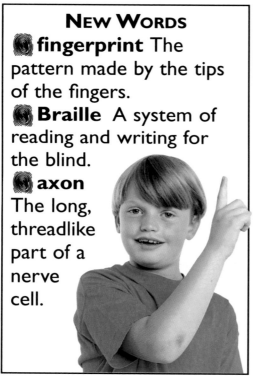 Our hands and the soles of our feet have many nerve endings. They have skin up to 1/8 inch (3 mm) thick, which is much thicker than on other parts of the body.

▽ **Nerve endings** lie just beneath the surface of the skin. They send messages along threadlike axons.

Nerve signals can travel through the body at 240 mph (400 kph), so they reach the brain very quickly!

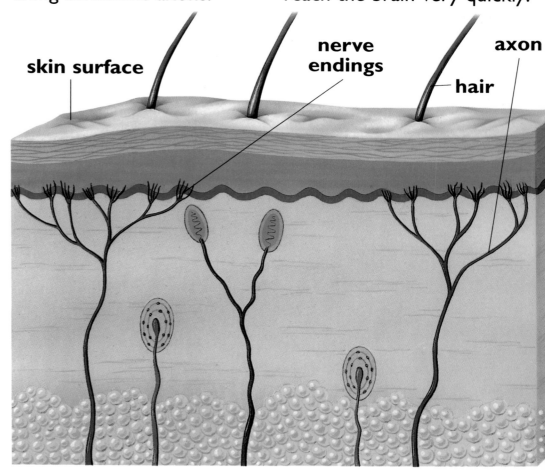

skin surface   nerve endings   axon

hair

Touching

When we touch things, nerve endings just under the surface of the skin send messages to the brain through the central nervous system. The brain interprets the messages, and we feel things.

Our nerves can help us feel hardness, softness and sharpness, for example. We can also feel heat and cold. Some parts of the body, such as our fingertips, have many more nerve endings than others.

▽ **Our sense of touch** gives us information about the world. It allows us to learn about things around us without seeing them.

TOUCHY-FEELY GAME

Put lots of separate objects in a bag. Choose things that feel different, such as an apple, an orange, a soft toy, a brush, a stone, a pencil, and so on. Ask a friend to put one hand in the bag and guess what they can feel. Then ask your friend to put different things in the bag for you to have your turn.

How Babies Grow

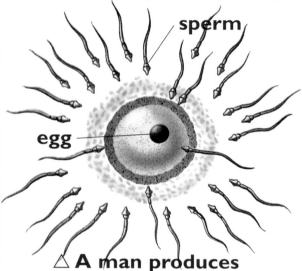

△ **A man produces sperm**. When one sperm joins up with a woman's egg, the fertilized egg starts to grow and develop into a baby.

Each of us began life as a tiny cell inside our mother's body. One of our father's cells joined up with one of our mother's egg cells. The egg cell then grew, to make a baby.

Babies grow in the part of a woman's body called the womb. It takes about nine months for the cell to grow into a fully formed baby. As the baby gets bigger, the mother's womb stretches to make room for it. When it is ready, the mother's muscles start to push the baby out of her body and into the world.

◁ **Doctors** can check on a baby's health before it is born. They use a special scanner that shows a picture of the inside of the mother's womb. They can even see whether the baby is a boy or a girl.

A baby is about 20 inches (50 cm) long at birth. When she gives birth, the mother is usually helped by a special doctor, called an obstetrician.

▷ **These are the organs** which help a woman and a man make a baby. Eggs are made in a woman's ovaries. They then move down the fallopian tubes next to the womb. Sperm is made in a man's testicles, and moves through tubes to the penis.

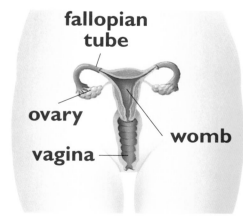

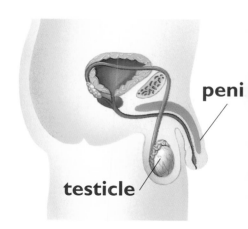

▷ **When children are born** to the same parents, they are brothers or sisters. Sometimes a mother has two babies at the same time, and these are called twins. They share the same birthday throughout their lives.

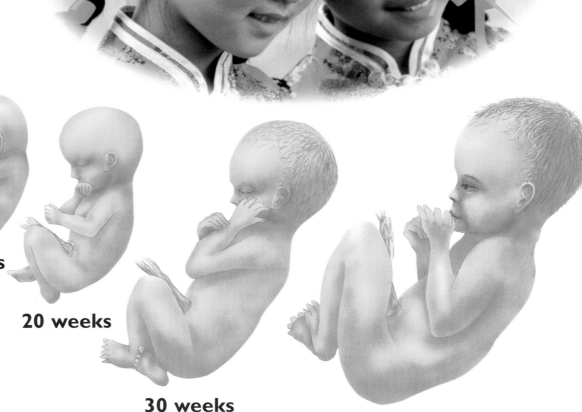

weeks

8 weeks

12 weeks

20 weeks

30 weeks

40 weeks

△ **A baby grows** very quickly in a bag of warm liquid in the womb. After eight weeks, it is about 1 3/4 inches (4 cm) long and has all its important body organs.

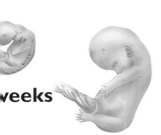
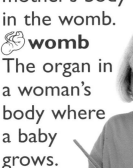

Inside the womb a baby floats in a watery fluid. It gets food and oxygen from its mother's body, through a tube called the umbilical cord.

▽ **The mother** may give birth in a hospital, or at home. When the baby's umbilical cord is cut, it leaves a mark called the navel, or belly button.

Growing Up

Babies need a lot of love and care, because they cannot look after themselves. But babies grow and learn very quickly, so that, as young children, they can soon do a lot of things for themselves.

By the time a child is two years old, it is about half the height it will be as an adult. Young children go on growing quickly, reaching three quarters of their adult height by the age of about nine.

Children go on to become teenagers and then young adults. As adults they may leave their parents and eventually have children of their own.

△ **A baby** learns a huge amount in a short space of time. She learns to use her hands and feet to crawl and push herself up, before standing up and taking her first proper steps.

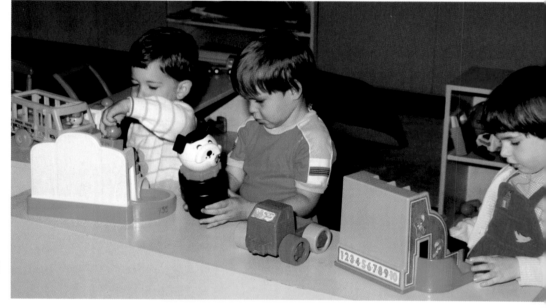

NEW WORDS

college A place where you can go after school to continue with your learning.

retire To stop working— usually when you are old.

△ **Children** love playing, and they learn a lot through play. When children play together, they learn about helping each other as well as about the objects and materials they play with.

As people grow older, their bodies' cells cannot replace themselves so quickly. This means it takes longer for damaged parts of the body to get better.

How tall?
The world's tallest person was Robert Wadlow (1918-1940). He was taller than most adults by the age of ten, and finally reached a height of 8 feet, 11 inches (2.72 m). That is over half as tall again as many grown-up people.

◁ **Children playing at the beach** have a lot of fun. At the same time (and without realizing it), they learn a great deal about themselves and the world around them.

The oldest person in the world was Jeanne Calment, who was born in France in 1875. She died in 1997, at the age of 122 years.

▽ **Old people** usually retire from their jobs, as their bodies start to slow down. Then they may be able to spend time doing things they enjoy, such as woodworking or gardening.

Teenagers are young adults. When they finish school, they may go on to a college. They start to make their own decisions and become independent.

△ **Most children** enjoy going to school where they make friends with other children and have fun. They also learn about many interesting things and play lots of games.

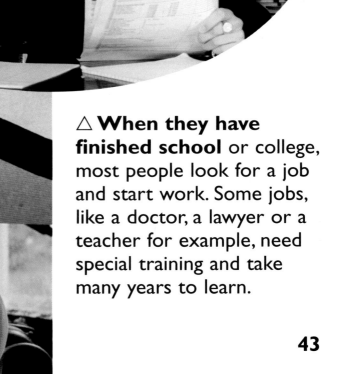

△ **When they have finished school** or college, most people look for a job and start work. Some jobs, like a doctor, a lawyer or a teacher for example, need special training and take many years to learn.

Keeping Healthy

To stay healthy, we have to look after our bodies. We can make sure that we eat properly, get plenty of exercise, get as much sleep as we need, and keep ourselves clean.

Sometimes there is nothing you can do to stop yourself getting sick. But if you lead a healthy life, you will probably be able to get better much more quickly.

We can all avoid doing things that we know damage the body, such as smoking cigarettes, drinking too much alcohol, or taking harmful drugs.

△ **Exercise** helps keep our muscles, as well as the heart and lungs, working well. It also helps keep bones strong. But if you are not used to exercise, don't suddenly do too much.

◁ **Washing with soap and water** helps keep us clean and get rid of germs. You should always wash your hands after you have been to the toilet.

△ **Sometimes we need to go to the hospital,** where doctors and nurses help make us better again. If you were to break a bone, you would need to go to a hospital for treatment.

◁ **Flies and other animals** can spread germs and disease. That is why it is very important to store and serve food carefully, so that it stays fresh and is healthy for us to eat.

44

▽ **When we are ill,** the doctor may give us pills or medicine to help make us better. You must follow the doctor's instructions and never take pills without first asking for permission.

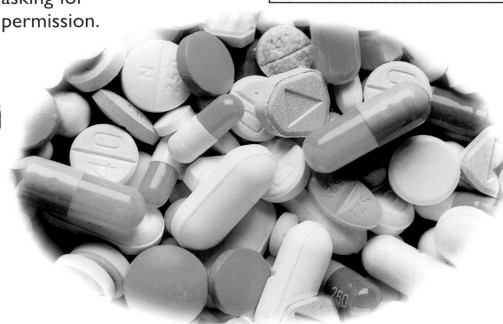

▽ **Many adults go to a gym** or a sports club to have a workout and keep fit. Dance exercises and aerobics are very popular.

Today we can be vaccinated against many diseases, either by injection or by mouth. Vaccination gives us a mild, harmless form of the disease and stops us getting it later.

Taking part in sport is an enjoyable way to get lots of exercise. Swimming helps to make you strong and supple, and jogging is good for stamina.

Doing dance exercises can help to make you more supple and will improve your stamina. For athletes, these sorts of exercises may be part of an overall fitness program.

Quiz

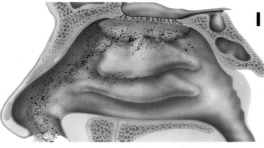

1. Which part of the body helps us to think and move? *(page 8)*

2. We are made up of billions of tiny living units— what are they called? *(page 9)*

3. What is the name of our framework of bones? *(page 10)*

4. Are you likely to be shorter or taller in the evening? *(page 11)*

5. Roughly how many muscles are there in the human body? *(page 12)*

6. Which muscle works together with the biceps? *(page 13)*

7. Which blood vessels carry blood away from the heart? *(page 14)*

8. How many liters of blood does an adult body contain? *(page 15)*

9. Does your heart beat faster or slower when you run? *(page 16)*

10. What do asthma-sufferers use to help them breathe? *(page 17)*

11. What vibrate in your throat to make sounds? *(page 18)*

12. Why do we cough? *(page 19)*

13. Which half of the brain controls the left side of the body? *(page 20)*

14. Where is the spinal cord? *(page 21)*

15. How much sleep do babies need in a day? *(page 22)*

16. What might you do when your body needs extra oxygen? *(page 23)*

17. Can different people have the same fingerprints? *(page 24)*

18. What are our nails made of? *(page 25)*

19. What are our pointed teeth called? *(page 26)*

20. What can you wear to make crooked teeth straight? *(page 27)*

21. Where does mixed-up food go after it leaves the stomach? *(page 28)*

22. What does the large intestine do? *(page 29)*

23. Why is fiber useful to us? *(page 30)*

24. What type of food are bread and pasta? *(page 31)*

25. Which part of the tongue tastes bitter things? *(page 32)*

26. Which nerve runs from the nose to the brain? *(page 33)*

27. Which bone does the hammer move? *(page 34)*

28. Can sound travel through liquids? *(page 35)*

29. What part of the eye bends light? *(page 36)*

30. In bright light, are our pupils big or small? *(page 37)*

31. What is the alphabet system for blind people called? *(page 38)*

32. Where do nerve endings send messages? *(page 39)*

33. In which part of a mother's body does a baby grow? *(page 40)*

34. What is another word for tummy button? *(page 41)*

35. How tall was the world's tallest person? *(page 42)*

36. How old is a teenager? *(page 43)*

37. What can help keep our muscles, heart and lungs working well? *(page 44)*

38. What does vaccination do? *(page 45)*

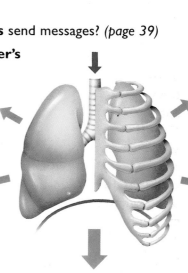

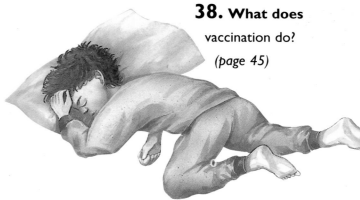

Index

ACKNOWLEDGMENTS

The publishers wish to thank the following artists who have contributed
to this book:

Guy Smith (Mainline Design) p9 (C), p10 (CL), p11 (L), p12 (CR), p13 (CL),
p14 (L), p 7 (BL), p18 (BR), p21 (CR), p27 (CR), p32 (CB), p34 (TR), p36 (BL),
p37 (CR), p38 (CR, BR), p40 (TL, BR), p44 (BL, CB);
Mike Saunders p9 (BR), p10 (R), p13 (TR), p15 (TR), p17 (TR), p19 (B),
p22 (L), p25 (TR, B), p26 (BL), p28 (R), p33 (BL), p34 (CL), p36 (C),
p37 (C), p41 (C);
Mike Foster (The Maltings Partnership) p13 (BL), p19 (TR), p20 (BR),
p22 (CB), p22-23 (T), p31 (CR), p32 (BR), p42 (BR), caption icons throughout;
Gillian Platt (Illustration Ltd.) p32 (CR);
Roger Stewart p35 (TL).

The publishers wish to thank the following for supplying photographs
for this book:

Miles Kelly archives p11 (TR, BL), p13 (BR), p15 (CL), p16 (TL, C), p18 (BL),
p21 (C, BL), p24 (TL, TR, CT, CL), p26 (TR), p29 (TR, CR, BL), p30 (TR), p31 (TL,
C, CL), p32 (TR), p35 (TR), p36 (BR), p37 (CT), p40 (CL), p41 (TR, BR), p42 (TR,
CR), p43 (TL, TR, CR, BL), p45 (TR, BR);
The Stock Market p 23 (TL), p29 (BL), p35 (B), p38 (TR), p44 (CR);
Patrick Spillane (Creative Vision) p18 (CR), p 27 (BL), p33 (T);
Science Photo Library p33 (C);
Tony Stone Images p11 (CR);
All model photography by **Mike Perry at David Lipson Photography Ltd.**

Models in this series:
Lisa Anness, Sophie Clark, Alison Cobb, Edward Delaney, Elizabeth Fallas, Ryan
French, Luke Gilder, Lauren May Headley, Christie Hooper, Caroline Kelly, Alice
McGhee, Daniel Melling, Ryan Ouyeyemi, Aaron Phipps, Eriko Sato, Jack Wallace.

Clothes for model photography supplied by:
Adams Children's Wear